Charles Lindbergh

Terry Barber

FAMOUS
FIRSTS
SERIES

Charles Lindbergh is published by
Grass Roots Press, a division of Literacy Services of Canada Ltd.

PHONE 1–888–303–3213
WEBSITE www.literacyservices.com

ACKNOWLEDGEMENTS

We acknowledge the financial support of the Government of Canada through the Book Publishing Industry Development Program (BPIDP) for our publishing activities.

We acknowledge the support of
the Alberta Foundation for the Arts
for our publishing programs.

Editor: Dr. Pat Campbell
Image research: Dr. Pat Campbell
Book design: Lara Minja, Lime Design Inc.
Book layout: Andrée-Ann Thivierge, jellyfish design

Library and Archives Canada Cataloguing in Publication

Barber, Terry, date
        Charles Lindbergh / Terry Barber.

(Famous Firsts series)
ISBN 978-1-894593-64-9

        1. Lindbergh, Charles A. (Charles Augustus), 1902-1974.
2. Air pilots--United States--Biography. 3. Readers for new literates. I. Title.

PE1126.N43B3643 2007   428.6'2   C2007-902784-9

Printed in Canada.

Contents

The Lesson 5

Early Years 11

The Prize 15

The Spirit of St. Louis 21

The Flight 25

The Hero 33

The Crime of the Century 39

Later Years 43

Glossary 46

Talking About the Book 47

The boy cannot swim very well.

The Lesson

The boy is in deep water. He cannot swim very well. The boy could drown. The father knows his son could drown. The father does not help him. The boy gets out of the deep water by himself.

The boy and his dog.

The boy and his father.

The Lesson

The father teaches the boy a lesson. The father says: "One boy is a boy. Two boys are half a boy. Three boys are no boy at all." The boy learns from this. The boy learns that he cannot depend too much on others.

Charles Lindbergh, 1909.

The Lesson

The boy never forgets this lesson. He learns that he can make it on his own. The boy gains a belief in himself. The boy knows that he must depend on himself. The boy is Charles Lindbergh.

Charles Lindbergh floats on a raft.

Early Years

Charles Lindbergh is born in 1902. He grows up in a place called Little Falls. Charles lives near the river. He loves nature. He likes to hunt and fish. He likes to build and play on rafts.

Charles likes to dream in a field.

Early Years

As a boy, Charles likes to dream. He lies on his back in a field. He looks at the clouds. He dreams about flying a plane. He wants to "ride on the wind and be part of the sky." One day, Charles will get his wish.

Raymond Orteig offers a $25,000 prize.

The Prize

In 1919, a rich man offers a prize. He offers $25,000. The prize is for the first pilot who flies from New York City to Paris. By 1926, no one has won the prize.

Lindbergh flies a U.S. Air Mail plane, 1926.

The Prize

It is 1926. Charles Lindbergh is living his dream. He has been a pilot for four years. Lindbergh has spent about 2,000 hours in the air. Lindbergh wants the $25,000 prize.

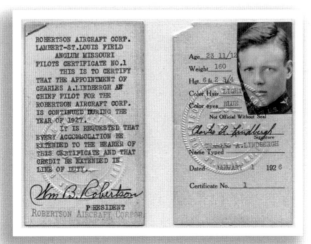

Lindbergh's pilot's license.

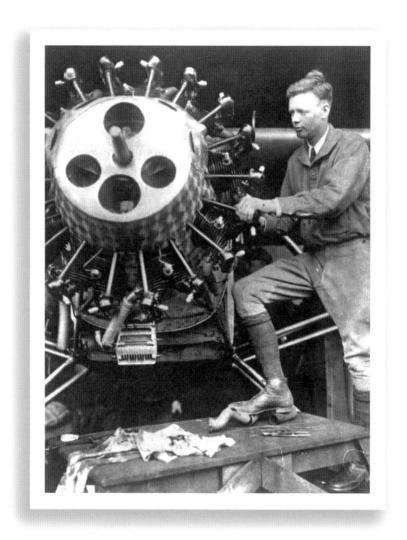

Lindbergh checks the motor in a single-engine plane.

The Prize

Many pilots want the $25,000 prize. Some pilots think they need a big plane to cross the ocean. They think the plane needs three engines. Lindbergh does not agree. Lindbergh wants to fly in a single-engine plane.

The $25,000 prize is equal to about $270,000 today.

Charles stands beside "The Spirit of St. Louis."
May 1927.

The Spirit of St. Louis

Lindbergh hires people to build a plane. It takes just 60 days to build. The plane is small and light. The plane is called "The Spirit of St. Louis."

Lindbergh plans his flight across the Atlantic Ocean.

A man fills the plane with gas.

The Spirit of St. Louis

The plane is built for a long trip. It is built to fly 4,000 miles. The gas must last that long. There are no gas stations over the Atlantic Ocean. "The Spirit of St. Louis" is not built for comfort.

The pilot's chair is made of wicker. This helps make the plane lighter.

Lindbergh flies out of New York.

The Flight

It is the night before the trip.
Lindbergh sleeps only three hours.
In the morning of May 20, 1927,
Lindbergh flies out of New York. He
wonders if one man can make the
3,600-mile flight to Paris.

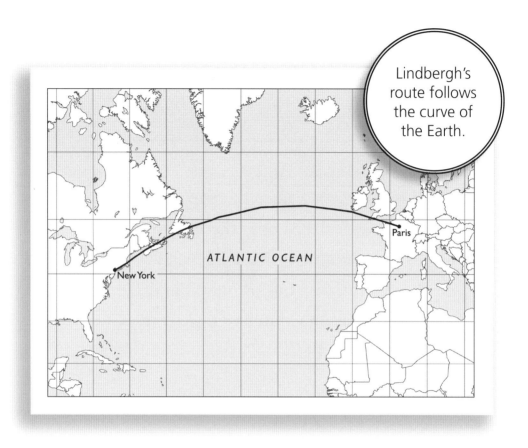

Lindbergh's route follows the curve of the Earth.

Lindbergh's route.

The Flight

Lindbergh has planned his route well. He follows his route closely. The trip across the Atlantic is very dangerous. In the 1920s, planes often break down. Lindbergh is risking his life.

Lindbergh is tired during the flight.

The Flight

The trip is hard. Lindbergh has to stay awake for about 40 hours. No one can help him. He feels tired many times. Sometimes, his eyes close. Lindbergh shakes off sleep and keeps flying.

During the flight, Lindbergh hears and sees "**phantoms.**"

Lindbergh is the first person to fly **solo** across the Atlantic.

The Flight

It takes Lindbergh 33 1/2 hours
to reach Paris. Lindbergh thinks
about two things. He wants to land
his plane. Then he wants to sleep.
Lindbergh does not know what waits
for him in Paris. Over 100,000 people
wait for Lindbergh to land.

Lindbergh lands just after 10 p.m. in Paris.

The police protect Lindbergh and his plane.

The Hero

Lindbergh shuts off the plane's engine. He fears people might get hurt by the propeller. The crowd will not leave Lindbergh alone. The police must help him get away from the crowd.

A crowd waits for Lindbergh to land.
June 18, 1927
St. Louis, U.S.

The Hero

Lindbergh returns to the U.S. He is a hero to the world. He uses his fame well.

Lindbergh travels to 48 U.S states. He promotes air travel. He promotes planes as a way to carry goods. He wants people to benefit from the plane.

Lindbergh and his wife, Anne Morrow.

The Hero

Lindbergh's fame is also a **burden**. The public wants to know all about him. The public wants to know all about his wife. People do not leave his family alone. Lindbergh does not like this part of fame.

Lindbergh marries Anne Morrow in May 1929. They have six children.

Charles
A. Lindbergh
Jr. is born on
June 22, 1930.

Charles A. Lindbergh Jr. is the
first-born son of Charles and Anne.

The Crime
of the Century

Lindbergh's fame leads to a sad time for his family. It is the evening of March 1, 1932. The Lindberghs' son is in bed. A man climbs up a ladder to the child's bedroom. The man takes the child from his crib.

The scene of the crime.

Bruno Hauptmann is found guilty of murder. He is sentenced to death.

Bruno Hauptmann wears handcuffs.

The Crime of the Century

The man leaves a note in the bedroom. The note says he will return the child for $50,000. The child is not returned. The child's body is found two months later. In 1934, the police arrest a man for the murder.

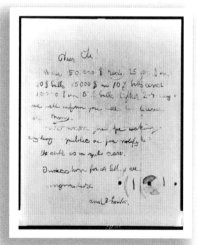

The **ransom** note.

The Lindberghs' home in Kent, England, 1937.

Later Years

The Lindberghs do not feel safe in
the U.S. They decide to move. For
a few years, the Lindberghs live in
England and France. They return to
the U.S. in 1939.

Charles Lindbergh, 1972.

Later Years

Lindbergh dies in 1974. People remember him as a champion of air travel. Lindbergh has shown the world how a person can live his dream.

Glossary

burden: a source of great worry or stress.

phantom: a ghostly figure that is not real.

ransom: money demanded for the return of a captured person.

solo: alone.

Talking About the Book

What did you learn about
Charles Lindbergh?

Lindbergh's father says: "One boy is a
boy. Two boys are half a boy. Three boys
are no boy at all." What do you think
this means?

What made the solo flight across the
ocean difficult and dangerous?

Why do you think Lindbergh's fame
is a burden?

Can you think of some ways that planes
benefit people?

Picture Credits

Front cover photos (center photo): © Lindbergh Picture Collection, Manuscripts and Archives, Yale University Library. **(small photo):** © San Diego Aerospace Museum. **Contents page:** © Lindbergh Picture Collection, Manuscripts and Archives, Yale University Library. **Pages 4 - 10:** © Lindbergh Picture Collection, Manuscripts and Archives, Yale University Library. **Page 12:** © istockphoto/konradfew. **Pages 14 - 21:** © Lindbergh Picture Collection, Manuscripts and Archives, Yale University Library. **Pages 22 - 23:** © San Diego Aerospace Museum. **Page 24:** © Lindbergh Picture Collection, Manuscripts and Archives, Yale University Library. **Page 25:** © Library of Congress, Prints and Photographs Division, LC-USZ62-68852. **Page 26:** © Bill Nelson. **Page 28:** © Lindbergh Picture Collection, Manuscripts and Archives, Yale University Library. **Page 30:** © Library of Congress, Prints and Photographs Division, LC-USZ62-70237. **Pages 31 - 38:** © Lindbergh Picture Collection, Manuscripts and Archives, Yale University Library. **Page 39:** © Library of Congress, Prints and Photographs Division, Clifford Berryman Collection. **Page 40:** © Library of Congress, Prints and Photographs Division, LC-USZ62-109425. **Page 41:** © Library of Congress, Prints and Photographs Division, LC-USZ62-120475. **Page 42:** © Lindbergh Picture Collection, Manuscripts and Archives, Yale University Library. **Page 44:** © San Diego Aerospace Museum.